GELATIN

SHOT

RECIPES

Mom Never Made

It Like THIS!

Volume 2

By: Lisa Frank

GELATIN SHOT RECIPES
Mom Never Made It Like THIS!
Volume 2
Lisa Frank

Layout & cover work: Lisa Frank
Printing & publication: Lulu.com
Website: stores.lulu.com/leezil

ISBN-13: 978-0-557-00179-8

Table Of Contents

Foreword

This time around I wanted to try something a little different. I had the idea to make pudding shots many years ago, but didn't have the nerve to try them. I experimented with the B-52 pudding shot after Volume 1 was published and it was a hit! There are some people who do not care for pudding, feeling it isn't as refreshing and cool as the gelatin, but those of us with a sweet tooth love them!

With the low carb trend surrounding us these days, I thought it might be fitting to apply the same principles to our shots. By utilizing sugar free gelatin and pudding mixes, I developed some treats that are relatively low in carbohydrates, but high in flavor!

The final section is non-alcoholic. I have several friends who do not consume alcohol, and truly enjoy when I bring these along to parties. They are also great options for kids. Instead of plain old gelatin and water, spruce it up and give them a new flavor sensation!

I have had several people inquire as to when this book would be published, but due to some personal issues, I had to continually push production back. Well, it is finally here and I hope you all truly enjoy it as much as my taste-testers have!

Gelatin Shot Directions

Gelatin Directions #1

Step 1	Bring water to a boil
Step 2	Measure out 1 cup of water into a large container with a pouring spout
Step 3	Add gelatin and stir for 2 minutes until dissolved
Step 4	Measure out remainder of the ingredients
Step 5	Pour ingredients into gelatin and stir well
Step 6	Pour gelatin into individual soufflé cups and arrange on a large tray
Step 7	Place lids on shots
Step 8	Place tray in refrigerator for shots to solidify, about 4 hours

Gelatin Directions #2

Follow Gelatin Directions #1, except in Step 1, instead of bringing water to a boil, boil soda in a microwave safe dish for 2 to 3 minutes (every microwave is different), and measure out 1 cup. Continue with Step 3.

Tip: All gelatin recipes use the 3 ounce size box.

Apple Blossom

1c. Boiling Water
1 box Green Apple Gelatin
1/2c. Brandy
1/4c. Sour Apple Schnapps
3T. Water
1T. Lemon Juice

Tip: Lids can be placed on cups while gelatin is liquid or solid.

Berry Delight

1c. Boiling Water
1 box Wild Berry Gelatin
1/3c. Raspberry Schnapps
1/3c. Strawberry Vodka
1/3c. Water

Blue Topaz Martini

1c. Boiling Water
1 box Berry Blue Gelatin
1/2c. Coconut Rum
1/8c. Blue Curacao
1/8c. Sour Apple Schnapps
1/8c. Sweet and Sour Mix
1/8c. Water

Tip: Four cup capacity measuring cups work well for mixing and pouring!

Calypso Cooler

1c. Boiling Water
1 box Peach Gelatin
3/8c. Spiced Rum
1/4c. Peach Schnapps
1/8c. Grenadine
1/4c. Orange Juice

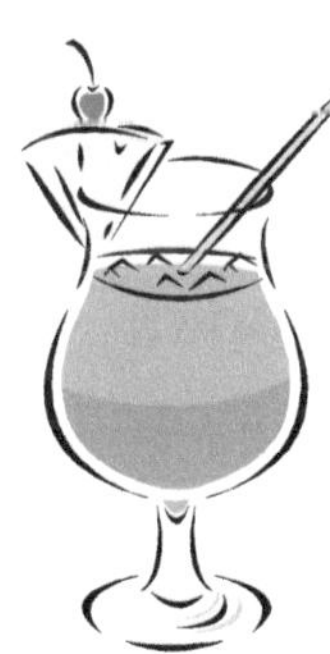

Cherry Daiquiri

1c. Boiling Water w/dash of Lime Juice
1 box Cherry Gelatin
1/3c. Light Rum
1/3c. Cherry Schnapps
1/3c. Water

Electric Lemonade

1c. Boiling Water
1 box Lemon Gelatin
1/8c. Vodka
1/8c. Coconut Rum
1/8c. Gin
1/8c. Blue Curacao
1/4c. Triple Sec
1/4c. Water

Georgia Peach

1c. Boiling Water
1 box Peach Gelatin
1/4c. Vodka
1/8c. Peach Schnapps
1/8c. Grenadine
1/2c. Pineapple Juice

Granny Won't Stop Screaming

1c. Boiling Lemon Lime Soda
1 box Green Apple Gelatin
1/3c. Sour Apple Schnapps
1/3c. Green Apple Vodka
1/3c. Lemon Lime Soda

Note: Follow Gelatin Directions #2 for this recipe

Hawaiian Punch

1c. Boiling Water
1 box Pineapple Gelatin
1/4c. Vodka
1/8c. Amaretto
1/8c. Southern Comfort®
1/8c. Sloe Gin
3/8c. Water

Hollywood Hottie

1c. Boiling Water
1 box Pineapple Gelatin
1/3c. Vodka
1/3c. Raspberry Schnapps
1/3c. Water

Lynchburg Lemonade

1c. Boiling Lemon Lime Soda
1 box Lemon Gelatin
1/2c. Bourbon
1/4c. Triple Sec
1/4c. Lemon Lime Soda

Note: Follow Gelatin Directions #2 for this recipe

Macaroon

1c. Boiling Water
1 box Orange Gelatin
3/8c. Coconut Rum
1/4c. Amaretto
1/8c. Crème de Cacao
1/4c. Water

Tip: If you don't have a steady pouring hand, a large syringe or turkey baster can be useful.

Mai Tai

1c. Boiling Water
1 box Pineapple Gelatin
1/4c. Light Rum
1/4c. Dark Rum
1/8c. Orange Curacao
1/4c. Grenadine
1T. Sweetened Lime Juice
1T. Lemon Juice

Melon Colada

1c. Boiling Water
1 box Pineapple Gelatin
1/4c. Light Rum
1/4c. Coconut Rum
1/4c. Melon Liqueur
1/4c. Pineapple Juice

Tip: If you have a party coming up, measure out and label cold ingredients a day or two ahead of time.

Peach Margarita

1c. Boiling Water
1 box Peach Gelatin
1/2c. Tequila
1/4c. Peach Schnapps
1/4c. Water

Tip: Always make sure you have all of the ingredients before you make the gelatin.

Purple Rain

1c. Boiling Lemon Lime Soda
1 box Raspberry Gelatin
1/8c. Gin
1/8c. Light Rum
1/8c. Raspberry Liqueur
1/8c. Tequila
1/8c. Triple Sec
1/8c. Vodka
1/4c. Lemon Lime Soda

Note: Follow Gelatin Directions #2 for this recipe

Purple Smurf

> ***Tip:*** It might be easier to double the ingredients, rather than trying to halve the gelatins.

1c. Boiling Water
1/2 box Cherry Gelatin
1/2 box Berry Blue Gelatin
1/8c. Vodka
1/8c. Light Rum
1/8c. Tropical Schnapps
1/8c. Blue Hawaiian Schnapps
1/2c. Lemonade

Raspberry Cosmopolitan

1c. Boiling Water
1 box Raspberry Gelatin
1/4c. Raspberry Liqueur
1/4c. Citrus Vodka
1/4c. Triple Sec
1/4c. Water

Red Headed Sister

1c. Boiling Water
1 box Cranberry Gelatin
1/3c. Jagermeister®
1/3c. Peach Schnapps
1/3c. Cranberry Juice

Tip: Keeping your spirits cold will help to set the gelatin faster.

Reggae Summer Splash

1c. Boiling Water
1 box Orange Gelatin
1/8c. Dark Rum
1/4c. Triple Sec
1/4c. Mango Rum
1/8c. Sweet and Sour Mix
1/8c. Grenadine
1/8c. Water

Sergio's Seven and Seven

1c. Boiling Ginger Ale
1 box Lime Gelatin
1/2c. Whiskey
1/2c. Ginger Ale

Note: Follow Gelatin Directions #2 for this recipe

Silk Panties

1c. Boiling Lemon Lime Soda
1 box Cranberry Gelatin
1/4c. Vodka
1/2c. Peach Schnapps
1/4c. Water

Note: Follow Gelatin Directions #2 for this recipe

Tip: Make shots with a friend! While one person is dissolving the gelatin, have the other measuring out the cold ingredients. Afterwards, while one person is pouring, the other can put lids on. You'd be surprised how fast the process goes!

Tangarita

1c. Boiling Water
1 box Strawberry Gelatin
1/2c. Tequila
1/4c. Peach Schnapps
1/4c. Mango Juice

Twisted Pina Colada

1c. Boiling Water
1 box Strawberry Gelatin
1/4c. Coconut Rum
1/4c. Pineapple Rum
1/8c. Raspberry Schnapps
1/8c. Sweet & Sour Mix
1/4c. Pineapple Juice

Tip: Place two different colored shots in the same plastic storage bag and simply label the outside of the bag.

Uptown Rose

1c. Boiling Water
1 box Raspberry Gelatin
1/4c. Raspberry Rum
1/4c. Pineapple Rum
1/8c. Raspberry Schnapps
3/8c. Pineapple Juice
Maraschino Cherries

> *Note:* Place a maraschino cherry in each soufflé cup before pouring the liquid into the cups.

Pudding Shot Directions

Pudding Directions

Step 1 Measure out half and half into a large container with a pouring spout

Step 2 Measure alcohol and add to half and half

Step 3 Add pudding mix

Step 4 Whisk for 2 minutes

Step 5 Pour pudding into individual soufflé cups and arrange on a large tray

Step 6 Place lids on shots

Step 7 Place tray in refrigerator for shots to thicken, about 2 hours

Tip: All recipes use the 3 ounce size box of instant pudding.

Almond Joy

1 1/2c. Half and Half
1 box Vanilla Instant Pudding
1/4c. Amaretto
1/8c. Crème de Cacao

> *Tip:* When pouring the pudding into the individual cups, a spoon & spatula will be handy to get all of the pudding out of the container.

B-52

1 1/2c. Half and Half
1 box Chocolate Instant Pudding
1/8c. Irish Cream Liqueur
1/8c. Coffee Liqueur
1/8c. Grand Marnier®

Banana Rum Frappe

1 1/2c. Half and Half
1 box Banana Instant Pudding
1/4c. Light Rum
1/8c. Banana Liqueur

Creamsicle

1 1/2c. Half and Half
1 box Vanilla Instant Pudding
1/8c. Vanilla Rum
1/8c. Orange Rum
1/8c. Triple Sec

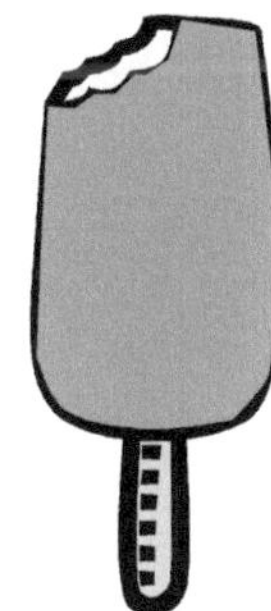

Hummer

1 1/2c. Half and Half
1 box Chocolate Instant Pudding
1/8c. Coffee Liqueur
1/8c. Light Rum
1/8c. Crème de Cacao

> *Tip:* You can use an electric mixer on low speed instead of a whip.

Mudslide

1 1/2c. Half and Half
1 box Chocolate Instant Pudding
1/8c. Vodka
1/8c. Coffee Liqueur
1/8c. Irish Cream Liqueur

Nutty Irishman

1 1/2c. Half and Half
1 box Vanilla Instant Pudding
1/4c. Irish Cream Liqueur
1/8c. Hazelnut Liqueur

Oatmeal Cookie

1 3/8c. Half and Half
1 box Vanilla Instant Pudding
1/8c. Irish Cream Liqueur
1/8c. Coffee Liqueur
1/8c. Jagermeister®
1/8c. Butterscotch Schnapps

Screaming Orgasm

1 3/8c. Half and Half
1 box Vanilla Instant Pudding
1/8c. Irish Cream Liqueur
1/8c. Coffee Liqueur
1/8c. Amaretto
1/8c. Vodka

White Russian

1 3/8c. Half and Half
1 box White Chocolate Instant Pudding
1/4c. Coffee Liqueur
1/4c. Vodka

Tip: When purchasing the pudding mixes, make sure it is INSTANT, not the kind that has to be cooked.

Low Carb Gelatin Shot Directions

Gelatin Directions

Step 1	Bring water to a boil
Step 2	Measure out 1 cup of water into a large container with a pouring spout
Step 3	Add gelatin and stir for 2 minutes until dissolved
Step 4	Measure out remainder of the ingredients
Step 5	Pour ingredients into gelatin and stir well
Step 6	Pour gelatin into individual soufflé cups and arrange on a large tray
Step 7	Place lids on shots
Step 8	Place tray in refrigerator for shots to solidify, about 4 hours

Gelatin Directions #2

Follow Gelatin Directions #1, except in Step 1, instead of bringing water to a boil, boil soda in a microwave safe dish for 2 to 3 minutes (every microwave is different), and measure out 1 cup. Continue with Step 3.

> ***Tip:*** All gelatin recipes use the 3 ounce size box.

Cherry Oh Baby

1c. Boiling Black Cherry Flavored Low Carb Malt Beverage
1 box Sugar Free Black Cherry Gelatin
1/2c. Black Cherry Flavored Low Carb Malt Beverage
1/2c. Water

Note: Follow Gelatin Directions #2 for this recipe, but in this case, microwave the malt beverage

Coconut Cruise

1c. Boiling Water
1 box Sugar Free Cranberry Gelatin
1/2c. island breeze™ Coconut Rum
1/2c. Water
1 Dash of Lime Juice

Tip: Use 3/4 ounce soufflé cups for a larger yield per batch, approximately 26 to 30

Key Lime Strawberry Daiquiri

1c. Boiling Water
1 box Sugar Free Strawberry Gelatin
1/2c. island breeze™ Key Lime Rum
1/2c. Water

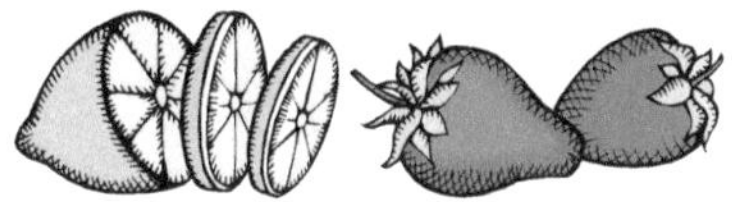

Lemon Drop in Carbs

1c. Boiling Water
1 box Sugar Free Lemon Gelatin
1/2c. Vodka
1/2c. Diet Lemon Lime Soda

Wild Berry Cola

1c. Boiling Water
1 box Sugar Free Raspberry Gelatin
1/2c. island breeze™ Wild Berry Rum
1/2c. Diet Cola

Tip: Line trays with aluminum foil or plastic wrap for an easy cleanup.

Low Carb Pudding Shot Directions

<u>Pudding Directions</u>

Step 1 Measure out whipping cream into a large container with a pouring spout

Step 2 Measure alcohol and add to cream

Step 3 Add pudding mix

Step 4 Whisk for 2 minutes

Step 5 Pour pudding into individual soufflé cups and arrange on a large tray

Step 6 Place lids on shots

Step 7 Place tray in refrigerator for shots to thicken, about 2 hours

Chocolate Berry

1 1/4c. Whipping Cream
1 box Sugar Free Chocolate Instant Pudding
1/2c. island breeze™ Wild Berry Rum

Coconut Cream

1 1/4c. Whipping Cream
1 box Sugar Free Vanilla Instant Pudding
1/2c. island breeze™ Coconut Rum
1T. Ground coconut

Island Treat

1 1/4c. Whipping Cream
1 box Sugar Free White Chocolate Instant Pudding
1/4c. island breeze™ Coconut Rum
1/4c. island breeze™ Key Lime Rum

Luscious Key Lime

1 1/4c. Whipping Cream
1 box Sugar Free Lemon Instant Pudding
1/2c. island breeze™ Key Lime Rum

Mixed Berry Cheesecake

1 1/4c. Whipping Cream
1 box Sugar Free Cheesecake Instant Pudding
1/2c. island breeze™ Wild Berry Rum

Tip: For a lighter, fluffier texture, whip the cream and liquor for about a minute before adding the pudding mix. Then whip for another minute. This will also provide a higher yield.

Non-Alcoholic Gelatin Shot Directions

Gelatin Directions

Step 1 Bring water to a boil

Step 2 Measure out 1 cup of water into a large container with a pouring spout

Step 3 Add gelatin and stir for 2 minutes until dissolved

Step 4 Measure out remainder of the ingredients

Step 5 Pour ingredients into gelatin and stir well

Step 6 Pour gelatin into individual soufflé cups and arrange on a large tray

Step 7 Place lids on shots

Step 8 Place tray in refrigerator for shots to solidify, about 4 hours

> ***Tip:*** All gelatin recipes use the 3 ounce size box.

Awesome Apple

1c. Boiling Water
1 box Green Apple Gelatin
1c. Apple Juice

Grape Goodness

1c. Boiling Water
1 box Grape Gelatin
1c. Grape Juice

> *Note:* These recipes are made with juice and make great snacks for kids - just pour into small serving size containers to set.

Outrageous Orange

1c. Boiling Water
1 box Orange Gelatin
1/2c. Orange Juice
1/2c. Lemon Lime Soda

Peach Passion

1c. Boiling Water
1 box Peach Gelatin
1c. Lemon Lime Soda

> *Tip:* Bulk food stores are a great resource for soufflé cups and lids.

Tropical Treat

1c. Boiling Water
1 box Pineapple Gelatin
1c. Mango & Passion Fruit Juice

Tip: Labeling shots with small color coded stickers helps to identify them better, especially if you have different flavors that are the same color.

Index 1

This Index is arranged by Gelatin and Pudding Types.

Gelatin

Pudding

Index 1 (cont.)

Index 2

This Index is arranged by Alcohol Type.

Index 2 (cont.)

Index 2 (cont.)

Vodka

Whiskey

www.ingramcontent.com/pod-product-compliance
Ingram Content Group UK Ltd.
Pitfield, Milton Keynes, MK11 3LW, UK
UKHW041834200726
13854UKWH00003BA/1129